Pictorial Archive of
PRINTER'S ORNAMENTS
from the Renaissance to
the 20th Century

1489 Designs

Selected by
CAROL BELANGER GRAFTON

Dover Publications, Inc.
New York

Copyright © 1980 by Dover Publications, Inc.
All rights reserved under Pan American and International Copyright Conventions.

Published in Canada by General Publishing Company, Ltd., 30 Lesmill Road, Don Mills, Toronto, Ontario.
Published in the United Kingdom by Constable and Company, Ltd.

Pictorial Archive of Printer's Ornaments from the Renaissance to the 20th Century is a new work, first published by Dover Publications, Inc., in 1980.

DOVER *Pictorial Archive* SERIES

International Standard Book Number: 0-486-23944-6
Library of Congress Catalog Card Number: 79-56178

Manufactured in the United States of America
Dover Publications, Inc.
31 East 2nd Street, Mineola, N.Y. 11501

Publisher's Note

Ever since the invention of the printing press in the fifteenth century, printers have used ornaments to fill space in page layouts and enliven the printed page. These ornaments can be distinguished from illustrations in that they have no connection with the content of the text, being purely decorative. This collection includes headpieces, tailpieces, dingbats, scrolls, trophées, lunettes, fleurons, calligraphic and heraldic devices, cupids and wreaths. It does not include certain other devices, such as borders, cartouches and decorative alphabets; these are featured in several other Dover Pictorial Archive volumes.

This book contains 1489 ornaments culled from over 30 sources. Many of the Renaissance and eighteenth-century engravings come from design compendia such as *L'Art Pour Tous* (1861–1904) and *Formenschatz* (1874–1894). Many of the more modern-looking devices derive from nineteenth-century type specimen books such as H. H. Green's *Specimens of Printing Types* (1852) and Zeese and Company's *Specimens of Electrotypes* (1885). These catalogues, made possible by the invention of electrotype around 1850, offered for sale to printing jobbers a tremendous assortment of printer's ornaments, as well as cast type in various faces. The cost of each ornament varied from fifteen cents to three dollars, depending on size.

Noted graphic artist and book designer Carol Belanger Grafton has selected these ornaments to reflect the broad range of styles favored by printers and designers during the last five centuries. Her criterion for selection has been the usability of a particular engraving for artists and craftspeople. The ornaments make an attractive complement to typography in books, letterheads and package design. They also may be used anywhere that small and elegant designs are required – in needlework and leathercraft, for example.

10

16

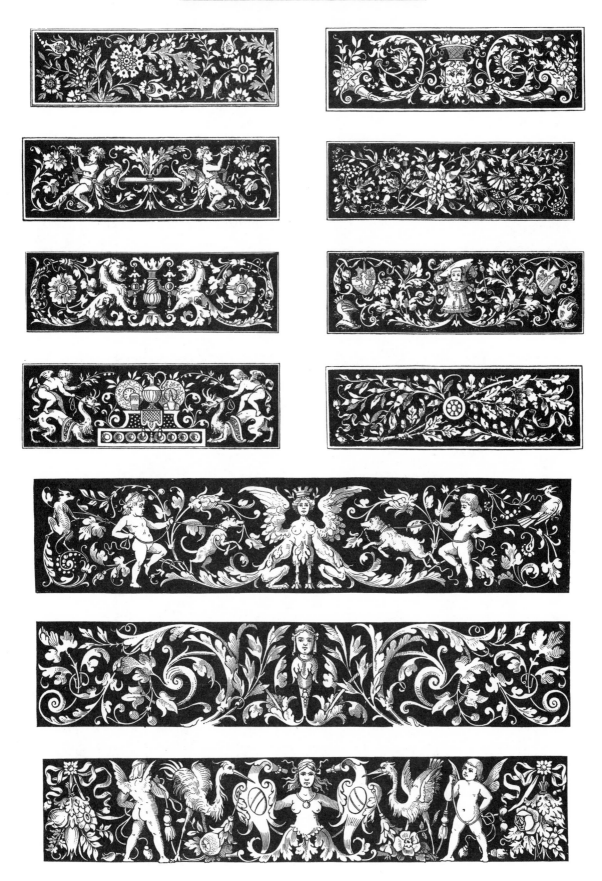

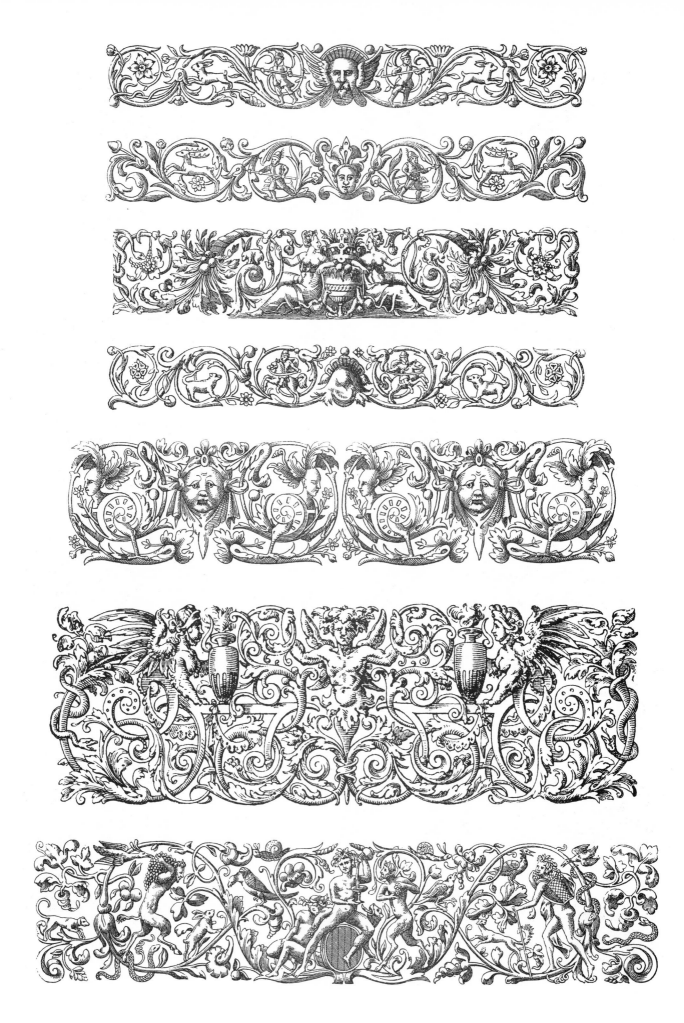

60

FINIS

72

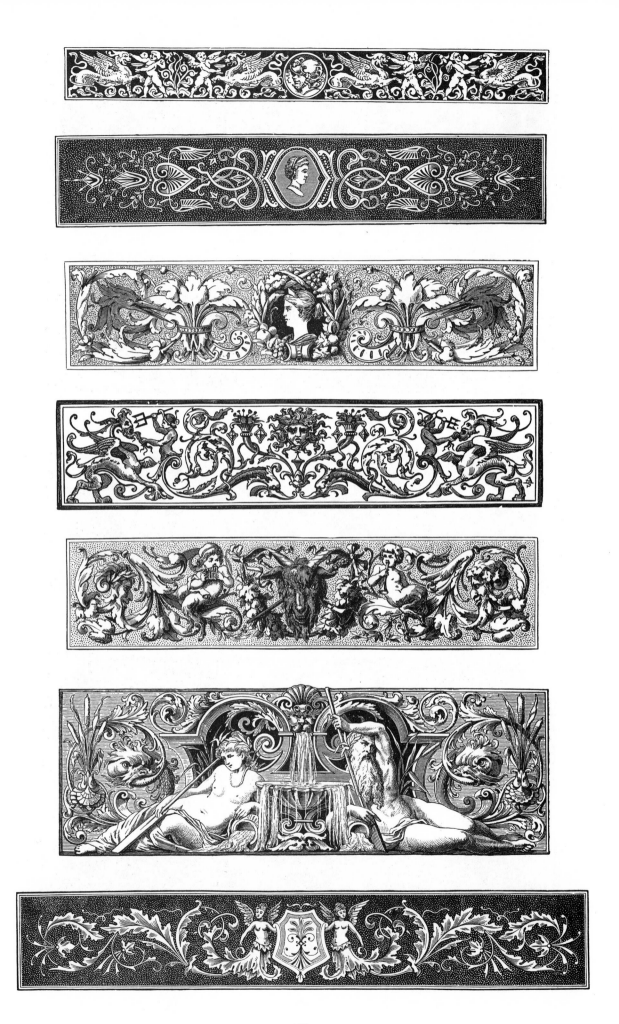

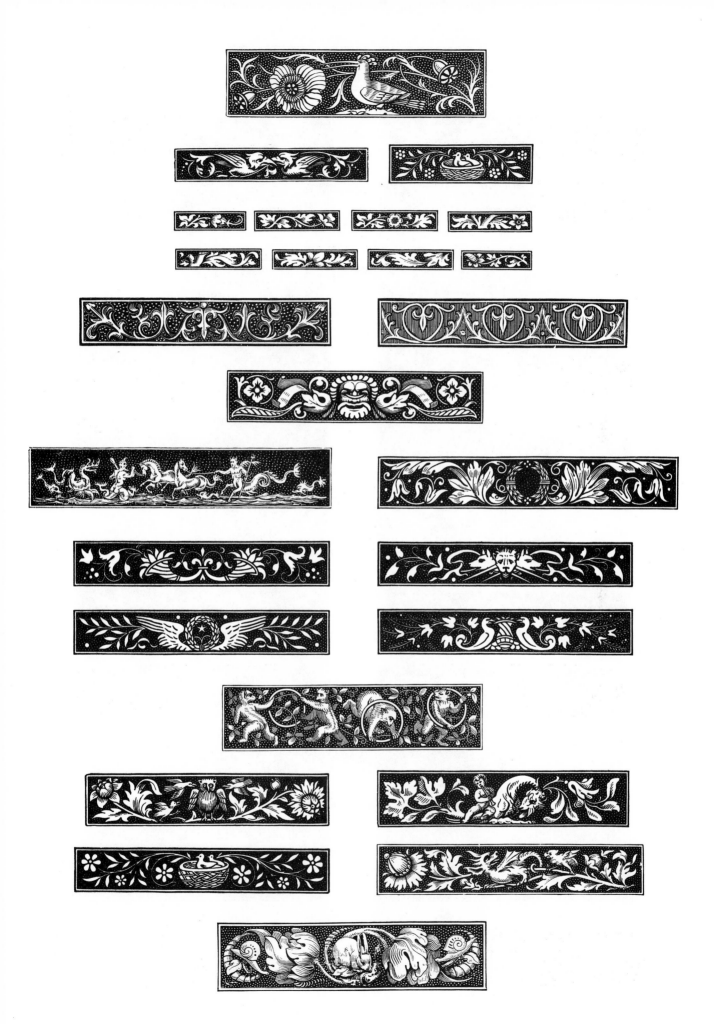

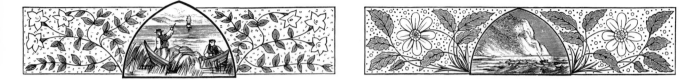

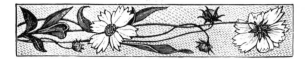

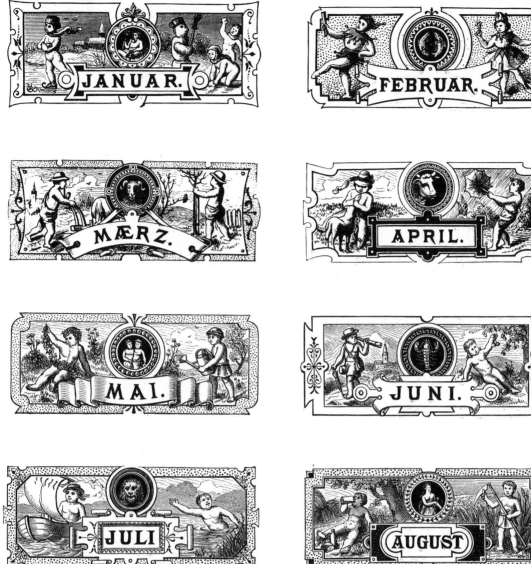

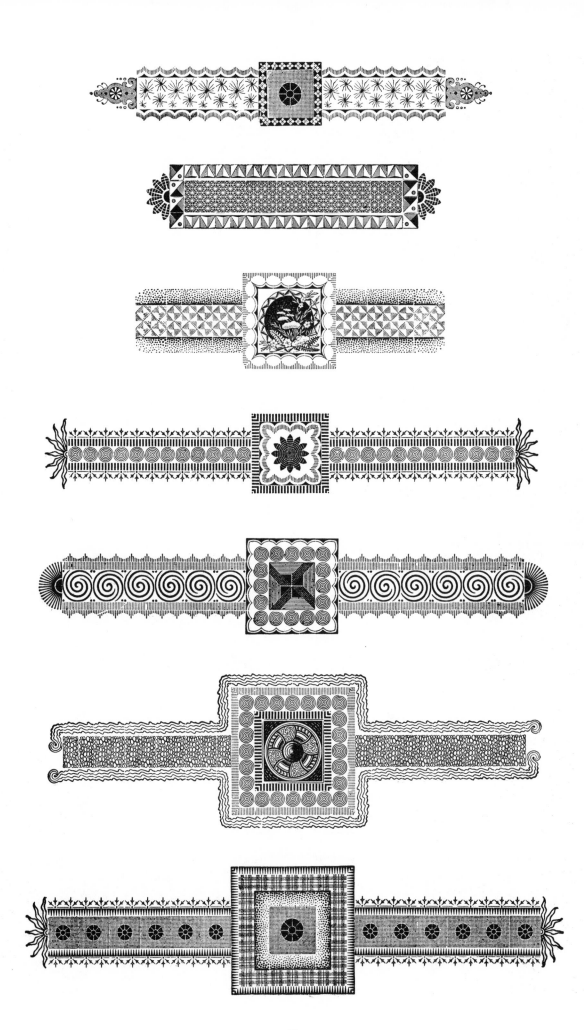

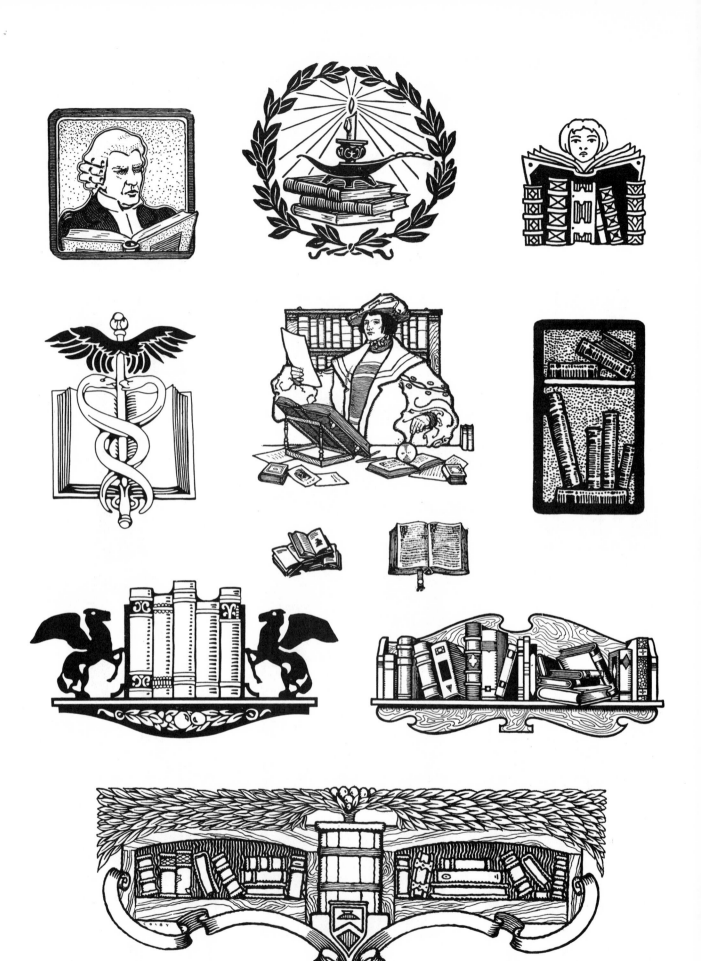

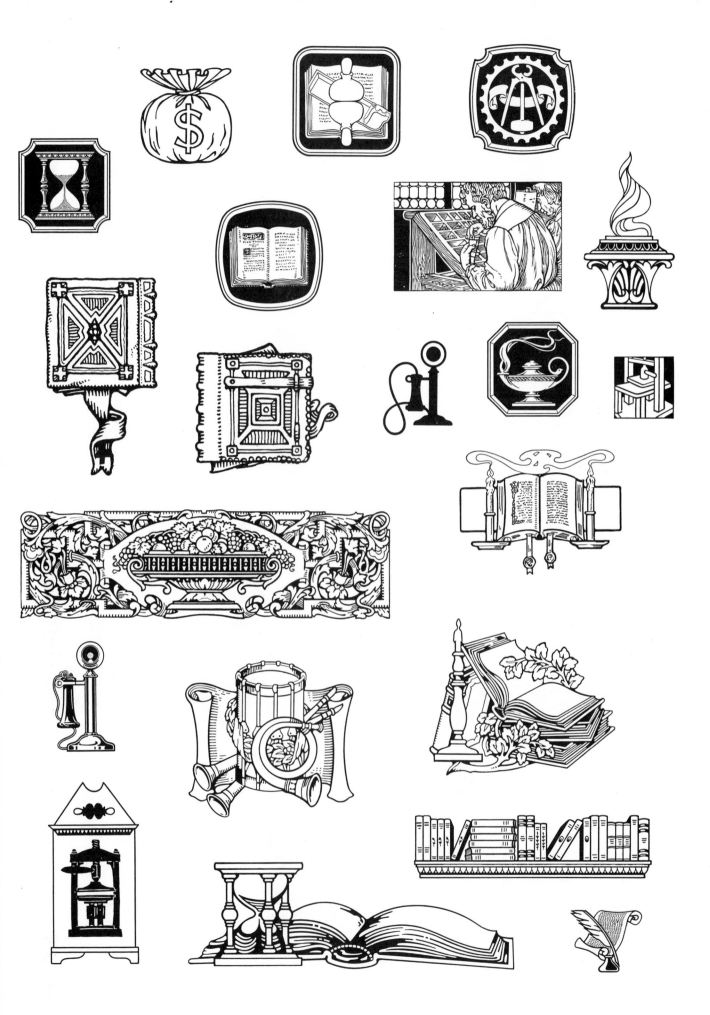

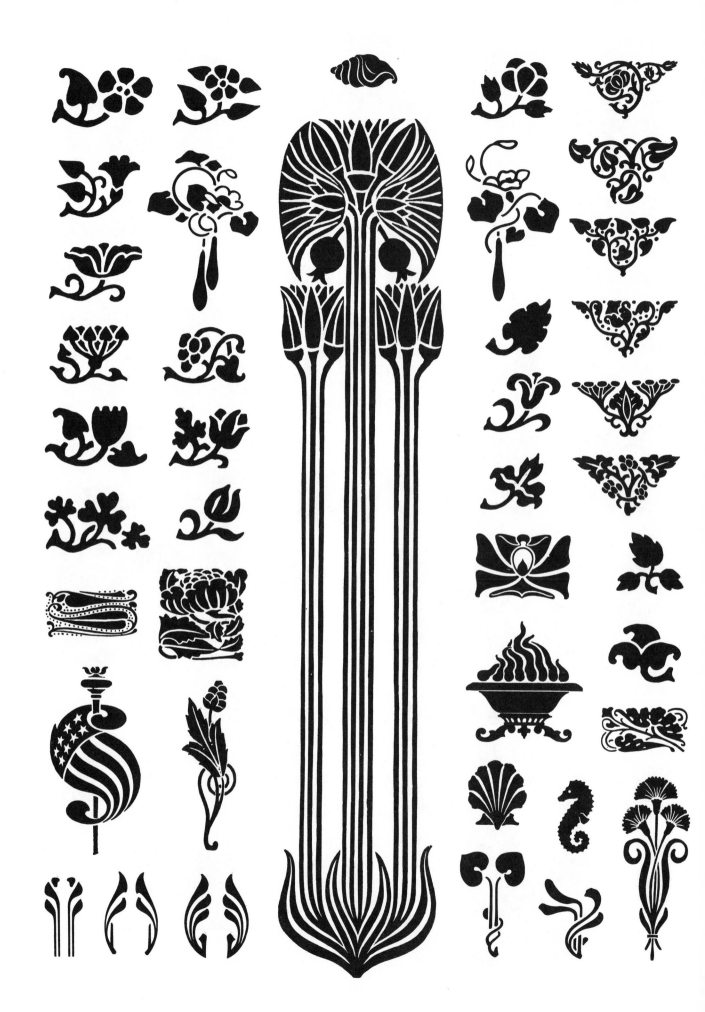

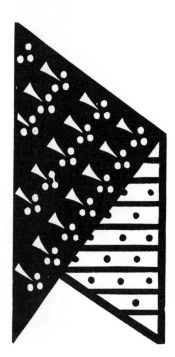